STILL MORE

KNOCK-KNOCKS,

Limericks and Other Silly Sayings

compiled by Laura Alden
illustrated by Diana L. Magnuson

created by The Child's World

 CHILDRENS PRESS, CHICAGO

Library of Congress Cataloging in Publication Data

Alden, Laura.
  Still more knock-knocks, limericks, and other silly
sayings.

  (Laughing matters)
  Summary: A collection of limericks, humorous
sayings, and knock-knock jokes on subjects such as
science, math, and animals.
  1. American wit and humor.   2. Wit and humor,
Juvenile. [1. Knock-knock jokes.   2. Jokes.
3. Limericks]   I. Magnuson, Diana, ill.   II. Title.
III. Series.
PN6163.A43   1986   818'.5402   85-27975
ISBN 0-516-01868-X

TABLE OF CONTENTS

Introduction

Knock-knock.
Who's there?
Savannah.
Savannah who?
Savannah you going to open the door?

No one knows for sure who told the first knock-knock joke, but we do know that knock-knock jokes were first told in the 1920's and 30's.

Because we don't all laugh at the same thing, there are many different kinds of knock-knock jokes included in this book to help tickle the funnybone of every reader.

Following the section of knock-knock jokes, you'll find limericks. The funny sayings known today as limericks were first written and told back in the 1800's. That's when a man named Edward Lear, a landscape artist, wrote and illustrated the funny, five-line sayings to amuse the young grandchildren of a friend. Here's one of Mr. Lear's sayings:

> There was an old man of Dumbree
> Who taught little owls to drink tea;
> For he said, "To eat mice
> Is not proper or nice,"
> That agreeable* man of Dumbree.

Although Edward Lear is the originator of limericks, lots of other writers, through the years, have taken to writing them, so the laughter continues.

Besides limericks and knock-knocks, you'll find tongue-twisters and other silly sayings — lots to laugh (or snicker) about — in *Still More Knock-Knocks*. Have fun!

(*original has word "amiable")

Name a Knock-Knock

Knock-knock.
Who's there?
Norma Lee.
Norma Lee who?
Norma Lee I don't tell jokes.

Knock-knock.
Who's there?
Ben.
Ben who?
Ben over and get the note I passed you.

Knock-knock.
Who's there?
Emerson.
Emerson who?
Emerson nice shoes you have on.

Knock-knock.
Who's there?
Amahl.
Amahl who?
Amahl shook up.

Knock-knock.
Who's there?
Osborn.
Osborn who?
Osborn in the state of Mississippi.

Knock-knock.
Who's there?
Agatha.
Agatha who?
Agatha headache. Do you have an aspirin?

Knock-knock.
Who's there?
Sabina.
Sabina who?
Sabina long time since I've seen you.

Knock-knock.
Who's there?
Mischa.
Mischa who?
Mischa a lot.

Knock-knock.
Who's there?
Wanda.
Wanda who?
Wanda play with me at recess?

Knock-knock.
Who's there?
Dot.
Dot who?
I Dot my eyes on you.

Knock-knock.
Who's there?
Mara.
Mara who?
Mara, Mara on the wall . . .

Knock-knock.
Who's there?
Beryl.
Beryl who?
A Beryl of monkeys.

Knock-knock.
Who's there?
Anita.
Anita who?
Anita quarter for a video game.

Knock-knock.
Who's there?
Nevada.
Nevada who?
Nevada saw you look worse.

Knock-knock.
Who's there?
Arnold.
Arnold who?
Arnold friend from Transylvania.

Knock-knock.
Who's there?
Samoa.
Samoa who?
Samoa old friends from Transylvania.

Knock-knock.
Who's there?
Hannah.
Hannah who?
Hannah partridge in a pear tree.

Knock-knock.
Who's there?
Ivan.
Ivan who?
Ivan my mommy!

Knock-knock.
Who's there?
Wendy.
Wendy who?
Wendy wind blows, the cradle will rock.

Knock-knock.
Who's there?
Darren.
Darren who?
Darren young man on the flying trapeze.

Knock-knock.
Who's there?
Sadie.
Sadie who?
Sadie Pledge of Allegiance.

Knock-knock.
Who's there?
Santa.
Santa who?
There's Santa my shoes.

Knock-knock.
Who's there?
Shirley.
Shirley who?
Shirley you won't forget me!

Knock-knock.
Who's there?
Ron.
Ron who?
Ron inside if it rains.

Knock-knock.
Who's there?
Olaf.
Olaf who?
Olaf you.

Knock-knock.
Who's there?
Barry.
Barry who?
Barry me next to the old oak tree.

Knock-knock.
Who's there?
Minerva.
Minerva who?
Minerva's wreck from all these knock-knocks.

Knock-knock.
Who's there?
Witch.
Witch who?
Witch way to the broom store?

Who's There?

Knock-knock.
Who's there?
Vampire.
Vampire who?
Vampire State Building.

Knock-knock.
Who's there?
Voodoo.
Voodoo who?
Voodoo you think you are?

Knock-knock.
Who's there?
Jaws.
Jaws who?
Jaws truly.

Knock-knock.
Who's there?
Ghosts.
Ghosts who?
Who Ghosts there?

Knock-knock.
Who's there?
Thumping.
Thumping who?
There's thumping green and slimy on your neck.

Knock-knock.
Who's there?
Goblin.
Goblin who?
Goblin your supper is not good for you.

Knock-knock.
Who's there?
Dragon.
Dragon who?
Dragon your feet again?

Knock-knock.
Who's there?
I.M. Igor.
I.M. Igor who?
I.M. Igor for your blood!

Knock-knock.
Who's there?
Dracula.
Dracula who?
Dracula milk, it makes you strong.

Knock-knock.
Who's there?
Spider.
Spider who?
Spider what they say, I like you.

Knock-knock.
Who's there?
Zombies.
Zombies who?
Zombies keep on biting me!

Here a Knock,
There a Knock

Knock-knock.
Who's there?
Could she.
Could she who?
Could she, could she coo.

Knock-knock.
Who's there?
Freighter.
Freighter who?
Freighter open the door?

Knock-knock.
Who's there?
Disc.
Disc who?
Disc is the program for your computer.

Knock-knock.
Who's there?
Thermos.
Thermos who?
Thermos be another way.

Knock-knock.
Who's there?
Wooden shoe.
Wooden shoe who?
Wooden shoe like to know?

Knock-knock.
Who's there?
Zone.
Zone who?
Zone shadow scares him.

Knock-knock.
Who's there?
Premium.
Premium who?
Premium gasoline—no knock-knock.

Knock-knock.
Who's there?
Atch.
Atch who?
Bless you!

Knock-knock.
Who's there?
Snowman.
Snowman who?
Snowman, it's a woman.

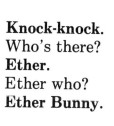

Knock-knock.
Who's there?
Ether.
Ether who?
Ether Bunny.

Knock-knock.
Who's there?
Cargo.
Cargo who?
Cargo "beep-beep" and run over Ether Bunny.

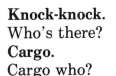

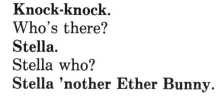

Knock-knock.
Who's there?
Stella.
Stella who?
Stella 'nother Ether Bunny.

Knock-knock.
Who's there?
Consumption.
Consumption who?
Consumption be done about all these Ether Bunnies?

Knock-knock.
Who's there?
Value.
Value who?
Value be my Valentine.

Knock-knock.
Who's there?
Ice pick.
Ice pick who?
Ice pick for the people of this country.

Knock-knock.
Who's there?
Police.
Police who?
Police! Open the door!

Knock-knock.
Who's there?
Ice cream soda.
Ice cream soda who?
Ice cream soda whole world will hear me.

Knock-knock.
Who's there?
Dishes.
Dishes who?
Dishes the end of the road.

Knock-knock.
Who's there?
Toothy.
Toothy who?
Toothy—the day after Monday.

Knock-knock.
Who's there?
Tank.
Tank who?
You're welcome.

Knock-knock.
Who's there?
Dimension.
Dimension who?
Dimension it.

Knock-knock.
Who's there?
Safari.
Safari who?
Safari, so good.

Knock-knock.
Who's there?
Someone too short for the doorbell.

Knock-knock.
Who's there?
Zsa Zsa.
Zsa Zsa who?
Zsa Zsa last knock-knock I ever want to hear.

Everywhere a Knock-Knock

Knock-knock.
Who's there?
Asia.
Asia who?
Asia going to invite me in?

Knock-knock.
Who's there?
Indonesia.
Indonesia who?
When I look at you, I get weak Indonesia.

Knock-knock.
Who's there?
Bolivia.
Bolivia who?
Bolivia me, I know what I'm talking about.

Knock-knock.
Who's there?
Uganda.
Uganda who?
Uganda get away with this.

Knock-knock.
Who's there?
Madison.
Madison who?
Madison the doctor gave me really works.

Knock-knock.
Who's there?
Savannah.
Savannah who?
Savannah you going to open the door?

Knock-knock.
Who's there?
Arizona.
Arizona who?
Arizona room for one of us in this town.

Knock-knock.
Who's there?
Uruguay.
Uruguay who?
You go Uruguay and I'll go mine.

Knock-knock.
Who's there?
Kenya.
Kenya who?
Kenya go to the movies?

Knock-knock.
Who's there?
Annapolis.
Annapolis who?
Annapolis a fruit.

Knock-knock.
Who's there?
Moscow.
Moscow who?
Moscow gives more milk than yours.

Knock-knock.
Who's there?
Kentucky.
Kentucky who?
Kentucky too well, I have a sore throat.

Knock-knock.
Who's there?
Cairo.
Cairo who?
Cairo the boat now?

Knock-knock.
Who's there?
Havana.
Havana who?
Havana wonderful time, wish you were here.

Knock-knock.
Who's there?
Fresno.
Fresno who?
Rudolph the Fresno reindeer. . .

Knock-knock.
Who's there?
Arkansas.
Arkansas who?
Arkansas more wood with my new chain saw.

Knock-knock.
Who's there?
Denver.
Denver who?
Denver the good ole days.

Knock-knock.
Who's there?
Ohio.
Ohio who?
Ohio Silver!

Knock-knock.
Who's there?
Troll.
Troll who?
Troll me the ball.

Knock-knock.
Who's there?
Jamaica.
Jamaica who?
Jamaica through the math test?

Knock-knock.
Who's there?
Iowa.
Iowa who?
Iowa dime to the library.

Knock-knock.
Who's there?
Yukon.
Yukon who?
Yukon have it!

Knock-knock.
Who's there?
Louisiana.
Louisiana who?
Louisiana boy friend broke up.

Laugh Out Loud Limericks

Teeth for Rent

There was an old man of Tarentum
Who gnashed his false teeth 'til he bent 'em.
    When they asked him the cost
    Of what he had lost,
He replied, "I can't say, for I rent 'em."

Fishing for Fischer

There was a young fisher named Fischer
Who fished for a fish in a fissure.
    The fish with a grin,
    Pulled the fisherman in;
Now they're fishing the fissure for Fischer.

Hippo Ballet

A hippo decided one day
That she would take up ballet,
    So she stood on her toes
    And said, "Okay, here goes!"
And fell back with a splash in the bay.

The Ostrich and the Thrush

An ostrich who lived at the zoo
Was bored with nothing to do.
    So he talked a thrush
    Into serving as brush. . .
And painted himself a bright blue.

A Horse, Of Course

A major, with wonderful force,
Called out in Hyde Park for a horse.
  All the flowers looked round,
  But no horse could be found,
So he just rhododendron, of course.

A Young Lady of Crete

There was a young lady of Crete
Who was so exceedingly neat,
  When she got out of bed,
  She stood on her head,
To make sure of not soiling her feet!

Scream for Ice Cream

There's a girl out of Ann Arbor, Mich.,
To meet who I never would wish.
  She'd eat up ice cream
  Till with colic she'd scream,
Then order another big dish.

The Bong Song

There was a composer named Bong
Who composed a new popular song.
    It was simply the croon
    Of a lovesick baboon,
With occasional thumps on a gong.

Three Little Birds in a Wood

There were three little birds in a wood,
Who always sang hymns when they could.
    What the words were about,
    They could never make out.
But they felt it was doing them good!

Fright by Night

A skeleton once in Khartoum
Asked a spirit up into his room.
    They spent the whole night
    In the eeriest fight
As to which should be frightened of whom.

Baghdad Boy

There once was a boy of Baghdad,
An inquisitive sort of a lad.
    He said, "I will see
    If a sting has a bee."
And he very soon found that it had.

Hall Fall Down

There was a young fellow named Hall
Who fell in the spring in the fall;
    Twould have been a sad thing
    If he'd died in the spring,
But he didn't—he died in the fall.

Amazon Sleeper

A sleeper from the Amazon
Put nighties of his gra'mazon.
    The reason was that
    He was too fat
To get his own pajamazon.

Hard Cider

There was once a young lady of Ryde
Who ate a green apple and died.
    The apple fermented
    Inside the lamented
And made cider insider inside.

Ride a Tiger

There was a young lady of Niger
Who smiled as she rode on a tiger.
    They returned from the ride
    With the lady inside,
And the smile on the face of the tiger.

Party Boy

There was a young man so benighted,
He never knew when he was slighted.
    He went to a party
    And ate just as hearty
As if he'd been really invited.

On Her Way Up

An opera star named Sapphire
Always tried to sing higher and higher,
    Till she hit a high note
    Which got stuck in her throat—
Then she entered the Heavenly Choir.

Liszt to This

There was a composer named Liszt
Who from writing could seldom resiszt.
    He made Polonaise
    Quite worthy of praise,
And now that he's gone, he is miszt.

Mysterious Men of Erith

There are men in the village of Erith
Whom nobody seeth or heareth,
    And there looms, on the marge
    Of the river, a barge
That nobody roweth or steereth.

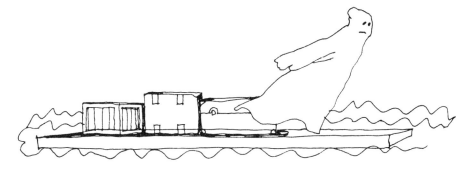

A Decrepit Old Gas Man

A decrepit old gas man named Peter,
While hunting around for the meter,
    Touched a leak with his light.
    He rose out of sight,
And, as everyone who knows anything
about poetry can tell you, he also
ruined the meter.

Woreham, Toreham

A thrifty young fellow of Shoreham
Made brown paper trousers and woreham.
    He looked nice and neat
    Till he bent in the street
To pick up a pin, then he toreham.

Cheese It

A cheese that was aged and gray
Was walking and talking one day.
    Said the cheese, "Kindly note
    My mama was a goat,
And I'm made out of curds by the whey."

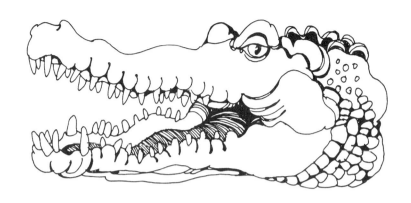

Blake in the Lake

A careless zookeeper named Blake
Fell into a tropical lake.
    Said a fat alligator
    A few minutes later,
"Very nice, but I still prefer steak."

The Wiz

The fabulous wizard of Oz
Retired from business becoz
    What with up-to-date science
    To most of his clients
He wasn't the wiz that he woz.

The City Man and the Kitty

There was a young man from the city,
Who met what he thought was a kitty.
    He gave it a pat
    And said, "Nice little cat!"
And they buried his clothes out of pity.

Poor Plesiosaurus

There once was a plesiosaurus
Which lived when the earth was all porous.
    But it fainted with shame
    When it first heard its name,
And departed long ages before us.

Lost Lady of Kent

There was a young lady of Kent,
Whose nose was most awfully bent.
    One day, I suppose,
    She followed her nose,
For no one knew which way she went.

Ruth Told the Truth

There was a young lady named Ruth,
Who had a great passion for truth.
    She said she would die
    Before she would lie,
And she died in the prime of her youth.

Mr. Manners

A rather polite man of Hawarden,
When taking a walk in his gawarden,
    If he trod on a slug,
    A worm or a bug,
Would say, "My dear friend, I beg pawarden!"

A Young Woman of Ayr

There was a young woman of Ayr,
Tried to steal out of church during prayer,
    But the squeak of her shoes
    So enlivened the pews
That she sat down again in despair.

A Man Mean, Wise, and Clever

There's a very mean man of Belsize,
Who thinks he is clever and wise.
    And, what do you think,
    He saves gallons of ink
By simply not dotting his "i's."

Ear and Eye

There was a young maid who said, "Why
Can't I look in my ear with my eye?
    If I give my mind to it,
    I'm sure I can do it.
You never can tell till you try."

Cold in Quebec

There was a young man from Quebec,
Who was buried in snow to his neck.
    When they said, "Are you friz?"
    He replied, "Yes, I is,
But they don't call this cold in Quebec."

Don't Steal the Dahlias

A woman caught stealing a dahlia,
Said, "Oh, you shan't tell on me, shalia?"
    But the florist was hot,
    And he said, "Like as not
They'll send you to jail, you bad gahlia."

A Fly and a Flea

A fly and a flea in a flue
Were imprisoned, so what could they do?
    Said the fly, "Let us flee,"
    Said the flea, "Let us fly,"
So they flew through a flaw in the flue.

The Old and the Gnu

One day I went out to the zoo
For I wanted to see the old Gnu,
    But the old Gnu was dead
    And the new Gnu they said
Was too new a new Gnu to view.

Eggs on Her Legs

There was a young girl of Asturias,
Whose temper was frantic and furious.
    She used to throw eggs
    At her grandmother's legs—
A habit unpleasant, but curious.

Silly, Silly, Silly

Hottentot Tot
If a Hottentot taught a Hottentot tot
To talk ere the tot could totter,
Ought the Hottentot tot
Be taught to say aught, or naught,
Or what ought to be taught her?
If to hoot and to toot a Hottentot tot
Be taught by her Hottentot tutor,
Ought the tutor get hot
If the Hottentot tot
Hoot and toot at her Hottentot tutor?

Prickly, Prangly
Peter Prangle,
The prickly prangly pear picker,
Picked three pecks
Of prangly prickly pears from
The prickly prangly pear trees
On the pleasant prairies.

Seven Swans a Swimming

Suddenly swerving, seven small swans
Swam silently southward,
Seeing six swift sailboats
Sailing slowly seaward.

A Boring Story

Once upon a barren moor
There dwelt a bear,
Also a boar.

The bear could not bear the boar.
The boar thought the bear a bore.
At last the bear could bear no more
That boar that bored him on the moor.
And so one morn he bored the boar.

That boar will bore the bear no more.

A Ghostly Poem
Three little ghostesses,
Sitting on postesses,
Eating buttered toastesses,
Greasing their fistesses,
Up to their wristesses.
Oh, what beastesses
To make such feastesses!

The Cassowary
Once there was a cassowary
On the plains of Timbuctoo
Killed and ate a missionary,
Skin and bones and hymnbook, too.

The Brown-Eyed Cow
I kissed the friendly brown-eyed cow
who gives us milk and cheese—
And now I'm in the hospital
with hoof and mouth disease.

Such a Deal

A little girl came into a grocery store and said, "Mom told me to tell you that we found a dead fly in the raisin bread."

"All right," said the grocery store clerk. "Tell you what—bring me the fly and I'll give you a raisin."

All in a State

If Mary goes far out to sea,
By wayward breezes fanned,
I'd like to know—can you tell me?
Just where would Maryland?

If Tenny went high up in air
And looked o'er land and sea,
Looked here and there and everywhere,
Pray what would Tennessee?

I looked out of the window and
Saw Orry on the lawn.
He's not there now, and who can tell
Just where has Oregon?

Mules

On mules we find two legs behind,
And two we find before,
We stand behind before we find
What the two behind be for.
When we're behind the two behind
We find what these be for,
So stand before the two behind,
Behind the two before.

Skunked

Once upon a time there were two skunks named In and Out. When In was out, Out was in. When Out was out, In would be in.

One day Out was in and In was out. Mother Skunk, who was in with Out, said, "Out, I want you to go out and bring In in."

In less than two shakes of a tail, Out went out and brought In in.

"How did you find In so quickly?" Mother Skunk asked.

"It was easy," said Out. "Instinct!"

Let's Make a Deal

Went to the river, couldn't get across,
Paid five dollars for an old gray hoss.
Hoss wouldn't pull so I traded for a bull.
Bull wouldn't holler so I traded for a dollar.
Dollar wouldn't pass so I threw it on the grass.
Grass wouldn't grow so I traded for a hoe.
Hoe wouldn't dig so I traded for a pig.
Pig wouldn't squeal so I traded for a wheel.
Wheel wouldn't run so I traded for a gun.
Gun wouldn't shoot so I traded for a boot.
Boot wouldn't fit so I thought I'd better quit.
So I quit.

Epitaphs

Here lies what's left
Of Leslie Moore—
   No Les
   No More.

Here Lies
what's Left
of Leslie
Moore—
No Les
No More

Here lies John Bun;
He was killed by a gun.
His name was not Bun, but Wood,
But Wood would not rhyme with gun, and Bun
would.

Here lies the body of Jonathan Pound,
Who was lost at sea and never found.

Two States

Two girls were quarreling one day
With garden tools, and so
I said, "My dears, let Mary rake
And just let Idaho."

An English lady had a steed.
She called him 'Island Bay'.
She rode for exercise, and thus
Rhode Island every day.

The Rooster and the Crow

I sometimes think I'd rather crow
And be a rooster than to roost
And be a crow. But I dunno.

A rooster he can roost also,
Which don't seem fair when crows can't crow.
Which may help some. Still I dunno.

Crows should be glad of one thing, though;
Nobody thinks of eating crow,
While roosters they are good enough
For anyone unless they're tough.

There are lots of tough old roosters, though,
And anyway a crow can't crow,
So maybe roosters stand more show.
It looks that way. But I dunno.

A Daisy on My Toe

I have a daisy on my toe.
It is not real. It does not grow.
It's just a tattoo of a flower,
So I look cool taking a shower.

It's on the second toe of my left foot—
A stem and flower that has no root.
I have a daisy on my toe.
My right foot loves my left foot so!

A Dog's Life

I've got a dog as thin as a rail.
He's got fleas all over his tail.
Every time his tail goes flop,
The fleas on the bottom all hop to the top.

TONGUE-TWISTERS

The big black-backed bumblebee.

A critical cricket critic.

The rat ran by the river with a lump of raw liver.

Double bubble gum bubbles double.

Nine nimble nobles nibbling nuts.

A regal rural ruler.

Which witch wished the wicked wish?

When does the wristwatch-strap shop shut?

The sixth sheik's sixth sheep's sick.

The wild wolf roams the wintry wastes.

Double Trouble

Sheep shouldn't sleep in a shack.
Sheep should sleep in a shed.

I never smelled a smelt that smelled
as bad as that smelt smelled.

Cows graze in groves of grass
which grow in grooves in groves.

I never felt that felt
like that felt like felt.

He ran from the Indies
to the Andes in his undies.